101

SURVIVAL

SECRETS

101

SURVIVAL

SECRETS

How to Make $1,000,000,
Lose 100 Pounds, and
Just Plain Live Happily

RICH HATCH

The Lyons Press

Designed by Compset, Inc.

Printed in Canada

10 9 8 7 6 5 4 3 2 1

The Library of Congress Cataloging-in-Publication Data is available on file.

ACKNOWLEDGMENTS

For life as I know it, I am thankful to the wholly heterosexual Thomas Thramann. Without his immeasurable intelligence and resultant love, compassion, insight, and generosity, I would not be half the man I am today.

I am thankful to Valerie Hood for her honesty and integrity and for her profoundly meaningful friendship. The intensity with which she has pursued and is pursuing health and happiness is uniquely admirable and, for me, remarkably inspirational.

Help came from many places in bringing this book to print, but *Survivor* is singularly responsible for introducing me to my readers and I therefore have many people to thank for their contributions. First and foremost, I thank Mark Burnett, not so much for his brilliance and drive (both of which are noteworthy), but for being the kind, thoughtful, caring man I've come to respect.

Thanks to Mom for saying, "Hey, I think CBS is putting together a show just for you!" And thanks to Dad for his sincerity and continued efforts. And thanks to my aunt Anna for her love and many years of trust and support.

Thanks to Craig Piligian, whose logistical genius made *Survivor* work, for caring enough to guide me to my manager, Alan David. Of course I am thankful to Kelly, Rudy, Sue, Sean, Colleen, Gervase, Jenna, Greg, Gretchen, Joel, Dirk, Ramona, Stacy, BB, and Sonja for sharing the island experience and a small part of themselves with me. I really want to thank the folks behind the scenes: Scott Messick (the director), the camera and sound crews, and the art department. I've never met more hard-working, professional, and cool people anywhere. Oh, and thanks to Les Moonves and CBS for picking up the show.

Separately, and most genuinely, I am thankful to three dynamic, caring professionals from CBS's publicity department: Chris Ender, Colleen Sullivan, and Michelle Hooper who, while beholden to CBS's interests, still seemed to maintain faith in who I am and supported me well beyond the scope of their responsibilities. Their kindness surprised me, and I am rarely surprised by people's choices.

Since winning *Survivor,* life has become bizarrely hectic and I owe thanks to many for their advice and guidance through what would otherwise have been an unmanageable maze. Thanks to Alan David and his assistant Mary Ann of Pure Arts for managing not just my career but my life, both calmly and brilliantly. Thanks to Amanda Laurence of Polaris PR for managing the unimaginable torrent of publicity associated with living a public life. Thanks to Steve Smooke and Creative Artists Agency for working to build a sustainable career out of my current good fortune. Thanks to Bob Walker and APB for handling my speaking engagements. And thanks to Stewart Brookman for managing the legal and contractual hurdles.

I owe special thanks to Chris Behan, my Rhode Island attorney, for his faith and competence—and to Joe Palumbo, for continuing the fight to make changes and make a difference. I also owe special thanks to my personal trainer, Jon Smythe, for his part in my living healthily and fit. And to Andrew Gold of Gold's Wood-Fired Grill and Café; I live a happier and healthier life as a result of his culinary genius.

Notwithstanding his politeness, I am grateful to my editor Brando Skyhorse for his keen perceptiveness, flexibility, stamina, and incomparable skill. Without him, this book would not exist. I am also grateful to my friend Tony Lyons of The Lyons Press for understanding me and agreeing to publish this book on an impossible schedule.

And finally, I'd like to thank all the ignorant bigots I've encountered in my life for helping me develop confidence and self-esteem by exposing the irrationality and vacancy of their views.

CONTENTS

PREFACE

My name is Rich Hatch. You might think you know me, and you probably bought this book based on having watched me win CBS's summer blockbuster show, *Survivor*. If you're anything like me, you're probably thinking you've got a pretty good idea of who I am and what types of things I'm likely to say in a book I'd write based on how I played that game, and how I achieved my success.

But what you couldn't get from that show is who I am in my everyday life, what I think, and what I believe about how people interact with one another.

I have nothing to prove. But I have a lot to say. And I want it to be possible for people to apply what I have to say to their lives in ways that are very, very practical. I want people to act so that they can see success, and once they see success, to have that successful action become routine and part of their everyday lives.

I hope your focused goal after reading this book will be happiness—happiness for you in your job (though you should quit if your job is pathetic, but more on that later . . .), with your partner, and in your life. I am successful because I am happy. And where does that happiness come from? Happiness comes from being challenged. And that challenge comes from being a little uncomfortable as often as possible so that I'm always learning and always growing.

I want my first book to be accurate, insightful, honest, helpful, and interesting. And I hope you picked up this book because you'd like to learn and to grow.

I'm not going to tell you that I have all the answers. But I do have a philosophy. And it works. It has worked for me and it can work for you. I hope that the survival secrets that follow help push each and every one of you farther than you ever thought you'd go; and I hope that in doing so you will get closer to achieving the happiness that you deserve.

CHAPTER ONE

THIRTY-NINE YEARS IN THE LIFE OF A FAT NAKED FAG

I'm a risk taker—there's no question about that. From my earliest memories, I've seen living life as an opportunity to explore, challenge, push, probe, provoke—to be constantly testing the limits of myself and others and asking why or why not.

All that started very early for me when, as a young child, I used to chase pigeons around a small park near our home, wondering about the way they interacted with each other and with me. For those of you keeping track of these things, I popped out on April 8, 1961, becoming the first of four children. I was the reason my parents got married, and it seems to me you couldn't find two more dissimilar people. My father Richard had three jobs. He worked at Eppley Laboratories as a technician making instruments with which to measure the sun, as a policeman, and as a lobsterman (which was my favorite of the three, and contributed to the development of my love for the ocean). My mother Peggy worked as a nurse.

For the most part neither of them was happy in their jobs. That made it difficult for them to be happy in their personal lives. This was a fundamental lesson I learned very early in life—and it forms the basis for my survival secret of *Quitting Your Pathetic Job* on page 39: one of the most important things you can do for yourself, your kids, your friends, and your loved ones is to BE HAPPY. Without happiness, you won't have the tools necessary to grow and to be successful, and you won't be able to help the people you care about find success.

I was a challenging child, both for my parents to raise and for people whose authority I was supposed to respect, for no other reason than that they were adults and I was a child. I was also a very sensitive child. Kids my age simply weren't thinking as much as I was about how their actions impacted others around them. I was always hyperaware of my environment. I was aware when people were picking on me for being overweight, and, much later, for being queer. I was aware when my mother was sad. When I watched my parents, I wished they could find a healthier way to interact. I remember feeling that I was different.

But I remember that feeling of being different as very empowering. I searched for ways to challenge myself to continue to be different. When things were expected of me, I had internal dialogues about whether or not to conform. I saw things more clearly and understood reality more accurately than many of the adults around me because I was learning another of my survival secrets: Learn to embrace your different-ness, and your imagination (discussed more fully on page 96). By exploring the ways you think differently as opposed to the ways you're supposed to think, you will be more likely to find yourself and therefore your happiness.

Despite my ability to embrace these feelings, they somehow weren't enough to give me lasting inner confidence. I was uncomfortable with who I thought I was, and I was uneasy within my own body, and ashamed of it. I remember not wanting to take showers after gym class in the worst kind of way. I'd sneak over to the sinks when no one was looking and wet my hair down, so it would look like I had already taken a shower. I absolutely didn't want to be naked in front of the other kids.

One time in sixth grade, though, my gym coach caught me wetting my hair, and said: "Go take your damn shower." While I was showering, some guy who was much shorter than I was, peed on my leg. Everybody laughed at me, and I tried to laugh it off, pretending that I was only a little embarrassed. But I was humiliated. And that's when I started to ask myself: Who am I? When I began to answer that question, I no longer felt humiliated. I learned to feel comfortable in my own skin. I'm sure this plays a role in why I'm now not afraid to be naked in front of fifty million people on television or to walk naked through Times Square.

But life growing up wasn't all about the humiliation of being peed on. I grew up in a quaint little town called Middletown in Rhode Island, which was part of a three-city chain of Portsmouth,

Middletown, and then Newport, which is where I live now. My child-hood house had woods to explore, a sticky marsh, streams to cross, and a large pond behind our property in which we'd play, fish, col-lect turtles, and watch muskrats, beavers, and pheasants. We always had dogs as pets (a beagle first, and then mostly German Shep-herds), and my father kept a raccoon for a while. We played kickball and baseball and hide-and-seek with the neighborhood kids. We went ice skating in winter. But the Hatch children were subject to more stringent rules than the other kids. We had to be home ear-lier, were given more chores, were forced to go to church. Swearing was forbidden in the house and only straight As in school was ac-ceptable. For the more important or repeat infractions, we got the belt.

One of the things I loved about growing up on an island was being so close to the ocean. I used to go spear fishing, snorkeling for quahogs (which I sold by the dozen throughout the neighbor-hood), and sailing with my father the lobsterman, with whom I hauled lobster pots. There's something about the ocean that makes you want to be near it and on it as much as possible, and I remem-ber spending hours and hours in the ocean with a mask and snorkel exploring the sea life.

One time, my "Uncle" Al (an oceanographer who was so close to my parents that I called him "Uncle") gave me a collection of sea life in formaldehyde from Narragansett Bay. I was utterly intrigued by what was inside—squid, sea anemone, clams, various inverte-brates—and spent countless hours studying them and looking up more and more about each of the specimens. After a while, I got really good at identifying different types of sea life and thought I was destined for a career as a marine biologist.

As I got older, I became even more challenging to raise and to deal with. I was adventuresome and unpredictable. In school, I got good grades but didn't fit in. I felt out of place, odd, disenfranchised. I couldn't afford the "right" clothes. I wasn't an athlete. I was worried about the size of my dick. And all my friends were girls. My parents divorced when I was eleven, and when I was fifteen I got kicked out of my mother's house because, as a single parent, she just couldn't handle me.

I moved in with my father, but we didn't have much of a relationship. I didn't feel like he knew or cared to find out who I was. There was so little connection between us that we rarely spoke to each other. I had to be home by nine o'clock on weekends, and like many teens who have difficulties dealing with their parents, I bucked the rules and regularly came home late. I even ran away once that year. With money saved from working at Mr. Sparkle Car Wash, I bought a car without my parents' permission or a driver's license and drove it around without plates. When my father caught me rolling a joint in my bedroom, he told me to get that stuff out of the house immediately. I responded with: "Can I keep it in the garage?" I got myself out of the house on my eighteenth birthday and quit high school. It had become clear to me that I was capable of managing myself better than my father could.

I moved into a motel on the island, and didn't know what I was going to do next. But a phenomenal teacher named Paul Mello, who taught physics at Middletown High (and still does), realized I had potential. He found me at the motel, I don't know how, and invited me to his home, under one condition: I had to go back and graduate. It was a challenge, so I agreed. I moved in with Paul, made up everything that I had missed, and graduated with the rest of my class, on time.

Paul also helped me prepare for the next stage of my life (or the next stage you're supposed to prepare for after high school): college. He helped me work on my application for Florida Institute of Technology, which was where I wanted to go, and coordinated my involvement in Horizon Bound, an outdoor program for troubled teens. While Horizon Bound is now defunct, I have set myself the challenge of starting it up again—or at least something similar to it.

The summer before college, while other kids were waiting tables or making out in the backseats of cars, I was spending twenty-some-odd days in the wilderness as a participant in the Horizon Bound program. We canoed down the West Penobscot River in Maine, hiked the Appalachian Trail, climbed Mount Khatadin, and even went rappelling off of cliffs! It was an extraordinary experience for me to go into the woods, to be challenged physically and to engage mentally with other people whom I hadn't met until then and to rely on them and work together and support one another and argue. Does all that sound familiar? I still go on these types of trips to this day; they teach me a lot about myself as a person, and I learn a lot from the other participants. I'd love to be able to share this opportunity with a new generation of kids who are at a time in their lives when they are trying to figure out who they are.

I moved down to Melbourne, Florida, in the fall for my first year of college. As much as I loved Newport, I couldn't wait to get off the island. I hadn't fully come to terms with being gay, and wanted to find a new environment where people didn't have preconceived notions about me. The challenge here wasn't to reinvent myself, but to BE MYSELF.

But college and I didn't get along, which ties in with another of my survival secrets about diplomas and degrees (I'll give you a hint: They're not important). It was hard for me to find meaning in the bureaucracy. Classes weren't interesting or challenging. Memorizing other people's ideas seemed wasteful to me and perhaps even harmful, since spewing oversimplified information back to professors stifled my creativity. I had thought I couldn't go much further in life without a degree. I had always been told that a degree means having an education, and that the only way you can get that education is to be sanctioned by an institution where you spend inordinate amounts of money for lessons that don't necessarily help you take risks or challenge yourself.

If you're a risk taker, and if you're willing to explore life in all its diversity, don't waste your time sitting in a classroom learning in the conventional way. I've been to six different colleges and had countless majors. It's safe to say that I learned much more outside of college than I ever did in a classroom. And more importantly, diplomas don't make you happy. Some of the unhappiest people I've ever met have a string of letters after their names and a wall densely decorated with framed diplomas.

That's when I decided to join the Army. Why the Army? Well, the Navy seemed like a much better fit, because I love the ocean, but it was rumored in our town that many of the people in the Navy were gay and I didn't want people to think I was queer! So I ended up at Fort Bliss, Texas, and became an assistant gunner on a Vulcan tank. I was fearful of failure during this period of my life; so much so that I performed well beyond what I thought I was capable of. My commanding officer noticed my strengths immediately. During basic training, he put me in charge of my platoon.

I learned a lot by being in charge. Mostly, I learned what a pain in the ass I can be. I was uppity, a stickler for detail, and kept trying to make people follow the rules. But I was doing it out of fear. And after a while I realized there wasn't any reason to set such high standards, to push so hard, especially with people who were satisfied with just getting by and who had no interest in becoming career officers. I realized that I didn't need to change the world. I needed to change myself.

My commanding officer, though, understood that I was ready for the next challenge and recommended me for West Point. Here was another challenge. It gave me the opportunity, as someone who was a little older and wiser than the average recruit, to observe how the academy was trying to indoctrinate us. It was interesting watching seniors, who were my age, standing in my face yelling at a lowly plebe like me, trying to get me to do what they wanted me to do. I happily smiled, and did what they said, but at a pace that I thought wouldn't get me into too much trouble. Here was another lesson, and as a survival secret it has served me well: I learned how to set up my own rules within the constraints of a rigorous environment.

I left West Point in January of 1985, about halfway through (at the beginning of my junior year) because if you stay past that point, you have to serve an additional five years in the Army. By that time I was more than ready for the next challenge, and that challenge was New York City! A friend of mine was moving into Manhattan where his sister, a flight attendant, had an apartment at 28th Street and Second Avenue. It was a tiny one-bedroom apartment, but the three of us decided we could survive there together.

I didn't have a good plan or much money saved, but I knew I wasn't willing to struggle financially for the rest of my life. My family hadn't been destitute, but we were on welfare for a while. Here was my chance. I knew I was bright enough to figure out a way to earn a decent living, especially in a place with unlimited opportunities like Manhattan. I had arrived at the Mecca for people who wanted to "make it," and I knew I was ready to earn my first million dollars.

My first job was as a carpenter. I had barely picked up a hammer before, but I saw learning how to build things with your hands as a challenge, so I dived right in and I loved it. One day, while I was doing some carpentry in a woman's house, I learned that she owned a company where I could work as a word processor, which I knew I would enjoy more than being a carpenter. (I could type over 100 words a minute back then . . . still can! How do you think this book came out so fast?)

Then one day I answered an ad. Jerry Rubin, the sixties activist, was hosting networking parties at a club called the Palladium where people came with their business cards and exchanged them in a clean, drug-free environment. Jerry may have been from the sixties, but he was wearing a business suit and was all business. He hired me as the host (or as the social lubricant) and my job at these parties was to get people talking, and help them exchange business cards.

During one of these parties, I met a young man named Tony Lyons, who was the head of security. We hit it off, and he hired me as a bouncer at the Palladium. And through Tony I met my best friend (and the man I named as my hero on my *Survivor* application), Tom. Tom is perhaps the single person I respect and admire most. He is my close friend, mentor, and role model. It would require a whole new book to explain his admirable qualities, but suffice it to say he encompasses those qualities that are most important to me in a friend—incomparable insight and singularly insuperable trustworthiness.

Speaking of incomparable insight, Tom is the man who coined the phrase "fat naked fag!" It was while I was on a camping trip with him and our friend Valerie Hood in Canada. I love to camp. For me, it's an important part of enjoying life and getting rejuvenated. The longer I spend out in the wilderness, the more powerful and rewarding the experience. We were climbing down a rock face (I was naked, of course, because I'm always naked), and Tom and Val had reached the bottom first. Tom looked up and got a view he'd really rather not have had, and said, "Wow, look at the fat naked fag!"

People have asked me if the word "fag" bothers me, or whether it bothered me when Rudy used the word "queer" to define me. Not in the least. I am queer—odd, different, gay. Words don't bother me as long as they're not malicious or mean-spirited. And when those words ARE mean-spirited, I take that as an opportunity to challenge people's perception not only of ME but also of themselves. Why do such people need to use these malicious words to attack me? Generally the answer is because they aren't comfortable with themselves.

Working at the Palladium was not only a very exciting time for me—I learned and grew greatly while working there—but it supplied me with two very important things: a cherished lifelong friend and an alliance with someone who would eventually publish my first book. These alliances are very dear to me, and if you haven't figured out by now that building alliances is an essential survival secret, then you didn't see the show!

Things got hectic in New York, as they often do. I had sublet seven different apartments in less than two years. Some were beautiful while others, like the one on Houston and Clinton in the East Village, were tough places to live—police and fire sirens, car alarms, flashing lights all through the night, foul odors, garbage strewn in front of the building, cockroaches, rats. And I had been working around the clock—at the Palladium and at my word-processing job, managing a limousine company and even working as a personal driver for Steve Rubell and Ian Schrager. Manhattan had swallowed me up. I wasn't working to live. I was living to work. I realized it was time to take a risk and go on to the next challenge. So I moved in with my cousin in Fairfax, Virginia, in yet another attempt to get a degree to help me achieve what I perceived as "success."

I continued to grow and develop as a person, and tried to help people around me grow and develop. I remember when my cousin found out that I was gay. She started to cry because she had the impression (from some movie) that gay people were maniacs who had midnight sex parties and smashed all the furniture. But she was willing to learn about me as a person, and she was willing to grow and change, so much so that we can laugh about it now.

While I was at college in Virginia, my professor Evelyn Hendrix made us give oral presentations in front of a large class. I was really uncomfortable with myself in front of an audience, and was amazed when she came up to me after my speech and said, "Rich, you've really got something." My reaction was: "What? Are you kidding? I hate speaking in front of people!" Speaking in front of a crowd was the last thing I thought I'd be good at, but since Evelyn was a corporate trainer herself, she asked me if I'd sit in on a training seminar the following week. Here was another challenge for me because I asked myself this simple question: What did I have to lose?

The next week, I took notes during her session—not on what she said, but on what she did. After the session, Jeff Neuville (the client) asked her if she'd be available to deliver the same seminar a few weeks later. She told him she wasn't available, but "he" was, and pointed right at me. I nearly crapped my pants! Those next two weeks I did nothing but prepare for this one-day seminar. I must have had enough material for a three-month conference!

And here's another of my survival secrets—I obtained, and utilized, as much information as I thought I needed to make myself comfortable with the topic I was discussing. Clearly, I wasn't going to make a living out of corporate training if I had to prepare two weeks for one day of work.

I did a great job my first time out. It took me a while to fully relax while speaking in front of large audiences, but I started to realize that the fear of public speaking, and that worry in general, was a complete waste of time (yet another of my secrets). What was the worst that could happen? I could say something really stupid and people would think I was a moron. Well, how would I correct the problem? I'd correct myself, people would realize that I wasn't a moron, and I would move on. Over time the ratio of preparation to delivery grew to a much more respectable level, as I learned more and more about how much information made me comfortable enough for the task at hand.

I succeeded in corporate training because I became intensely aware of why people attended the training sessions. I drew people in, got them involved. The learning process was both interactive and practical. I taught entry-level personnel, middle managers, and high-level executives basic to advanced principles of problem solving, teamwork, conflict resolution, and decision making. I worked for government agencies, nonprofit organizations, and large and small corporations. Jeff Neuville kept hiring me. People responded positively and recommended me to other companies. Before I knew it, I had my own company.

I worked very hard to get my business off the ground (more eighteen-hour days than you can imagine) and it was around this time that I started to gain weight. A lot of weight. I ballooned from two hundred and twenty pounds to three hundred and sixty pounds. I looked like a big fat moose! I couldn't fit into any of my old clothes and I had to work hard just to find clothes that fit me. Most had to be tailor-made. I had trouble getting into a taxi or finding a public bathroom that I could squeeze into and then have some reasonable chance of squeezing out of. I was depressed, overworked, stressed out, and not in control of my life. But most importantly, I wasn't happy, and as a result I was much more prone to overeating.

Here's where I learned another of my survival secrets. (And I hope you've noticed by this point that every one of the survival secrets that I've learned and have been able to implement effectively in my life has been the result of accepting a challenge and then pushing myself to understand and overcome that challenge.) I was fat because I *wanted* to be fat. I had chosen, consciously or unconsciously, to be a big, fat moose because I wasn't doing anything to change my situation.

But when I had made a decision to change the way I was living, to put MY happiness first, ahead of my business, and over anything else in my life that was distracting me, the pounds just melted away (Selfishness is a good thing! That's another tip on page 84). Of course, I have a lot of tips about how to KEEP that weight off (I limit bread, potatoes, and pasta, but I'm not going to give you a diet, or even tell you to diet because diets are STUPID [See page 49]).

I shed those pounds, and even though I periodically worked to control my weight over the next several years, I got control of my life and started looking around for the next challenge. I had been a corporate trainer for ten years, and I was financially and emotionally secure enough to consider supporting somebody else. I had always thought, even from my early teens, that I was going to grow up, get married, and have kids. But being a gay man made this a difficult challenge. I had just gotten out of a long-term relationship (broken off because Ralph, my partner of eight years, didn't want kids). I thought: Here's another opportunity presenting itself. I looked into adoption.

I was interviewed and learned about the adoption process. There was a nine-week session of classes to help you figure out if you were right for adoption, and if adoption was right for you. I went to the first class thinking that I might as well prepare to adopt, in case I decided it was the right thing for me.

Two weeks into the course, I was told about an emergency placement child who needed to be put into a single-parent home. Would I be willing to take him as a bridge placement until they found somebody? I said sure.

When he brought Chris over, the social worker told me that Chris's last family claimed he'd killed their cat. "And I think he probably did. Be careful," the social worker advised.

My sister, Sue, and I took my nephew, Jacob, and Chris to a playground and then to get some food. Later I drove Chris home and showed him my house and his room. I helped him unpack his stuff (which had been packed in garbage bags) and then asked him what he was feeling, trying to make the seven-year-old as comfortable as I could. I constantly observed him, trying to understand who he was and what was going on inside him. I discovered there was a lot going on. He's truly brilliant, and his intelligence is a saving grace (though when a child thinks he's as bright as Chris KNOWS he is, it can be a pain in the ass, too). It didn't take long for me to realize that Chris was perfect for me, and within a couple of weeks, I told the social worker to stop looking. Chris had found a home.

I am a loving father, and Chris and I have a great relationship. I say this even though there is a perception that I am a tough father, The Great Santini maybe, and that my toughness has spilled over into abuse. Nothing could be further from the truth. I travel for a living and sometimes have to leave Chris with a babysitter, which Chris then uses as an excuse to get his way (as any bright ten-year-old child would do). While I was on the island, I hired my sister's boss, Paul (an expert with behaviorally disordered children), to look after Chris. Paul moved into our house with Chris because I wanted Chris's routine disrupted as little as possible. Children do best when they're challenged but given set limits.

Unfortunately, my son took advantage of the situation and started to eat far more than he should have eaten—two breakfasts, two lunches, candy bars. He even repeatedly threatened Paul with going to the nurse and telling her that Paul was abusing him at home! So he had gained a lot of weight and I knew I faced another unique challenge in figuring out how to handle this.

We have a routine of morning runs; these are always at a comfortable pace, a pace that's slower than most people walk. I like running with my son because it makes him feel better than he's ever felt about himself. That's important for me as a father—to help my child develop self-esteem and confidence. When I got back from the island, Chris hadn't been out running with me in a long while, and when he decided he had had enough, he threw a tantrum in public. Now tantrums don't get very far with me. I even had to sit in with him in his second-grade class, sometimes three days a week, when his behavior was so disruptive that the school wouldn't otherwise let him stay with his regular class. It was definitely a learning experience that I'd recommend to other parents.

While Chris was in the push-up position and still throwing a tantrum, his arm slipped and he hit his forehead on the gravel. The pebbles left impressions, which amounted to nothing more than a little redness. I told Chris that his unacceptable behavior was not going to get him less running and that I would pick him up at the end of the school day and take him for an afternoon run. As kids are prone to do, when he was asked at school later that day if he wanted something (in this case it was some ice for his "bruise"), he said, "Sure."

By the end of the day, Chris was trying to figure a way out of the afternoon run, so he concocted a story for the nurse and the principal, which had them duty bound to report the incident to Rhode Island's Department of Children, Youth and Families (DCYF). The DCYF worker with whom they spoke said, "I recognize the name as the guy from the show. This might be important. Call the police." In my opinion, that statement was not only an irresponsible overreaction, but was actually abusive toward Chris in that it set an unfortunate chain of events in motion.

The principal called the police. By the time I arrived to pick up Chris at the police station, his bruise had become physical abuse. I was arrested, cuffed, fingerprinted, and put behind bars. I was outraged, and thought, well isn't this an interesting world . . . to go from a thirty-nine-day camping trip on a deserted island where I had just won a million dollars to being behind bars in my own hometown.

But all this happened after I had just returned from the island, when I couldn't tell anyone that I was the sole *Survivor*. But how did I keep it a secret, even from my own son? And how did I get to be on the show in the first place? And why did being gay help me win? Read on, dear readers . . .

CHAPTER TWO

MORONS AND BIGOTS AND BORES—OH MY!

How I Got on the Show and How Being Gay Helped Me Win

So how did I find out about *Survivor*? I got a call from my mother, who told me, "Hey Rich, CBS is putting this show together just for you." And I said, "Yeah, fine, Mom." Mom is always on the lookout for opportunities for me (I should pay more attention). Less than a week later, a friend from D.C. e-mailed me and said, "Hey Rich, I heard about this show that CBS is putting together just for you." The fact that both my mother and my friend said that this show was for me provided the impetus to check out the *Survivor* Web site.

I discovered my mother and my friend were right. It was a show designed just for me, because it reminded me of adventures I'd already experienced so many times. I've constantly sought this kind of adventure. In fact, I would have paid to go on *Survivor* without the incentive of winning anything. I had already spent a month in Maine as part of an outdoor adventure teen program, and another month in the tundra of the Talkeetna Mountains north of Anchorage, Alaska.

What do these types of adventures do for me? It's an indescribable feeling unless you've done it yourself. And you can, too. You don't need to go on a television show to find this type of adventure. You can go on outdoor adventures with friends or with troubled teens throughout the country, and though you may not become a celebrity by doing so, you'll find the rewards far, far more satisfying. Such experiences can be life-altering.

When you're stripped of all of the "noise" of everyday life and forced for the first time to listen to yourself, and to others, you get closer to discovering who YOU are as an individual. Relying on people for things that you're not used to relying on them for, working together to get things done, and dealing with people's emotions, whether you're hiking through the woods or across the tundra, you discover the possibilities and the limits of your abilities. And that's truly a wonderful and exciting thing, because it breaks through the stoic, stuffy barriers that we surround ourselves with in our everyday lives—barriers that prevent us from meaningful interaction.

But back to getting on the show. I had to fill out a lengthy application that asked a lot of probing questions. One of the most interesting questions was: "What types of people would you not want to have with you on the island?" My answer? "Morons and bigots and bores—Oh My!"

In addition to filling out the application, you had to produce a three-minute video. Initially, I produced it myself but then they extended the deadline for submissions, so I got it professionally produced. The video included pictures of me from West Point, shots of my beautiful hometown of Newport, and the (in)famous shot of me doing push-ups while my son, holding the camera, says, "Come on, Dad, do more push-ups! We need the money!"

There were over six thousand applicants. The odds were astronomical that I would even make it past the first cut. But I did. I was one of the eight hundred selected. Then there was a second selection process to narrow down the field to forty-eight people. I was flown out to Los Angeles where I underwent dozens of psychological tests and interview after interview after interview. During one test, I was stuck in a room with a camera for fifteen minutes and told I could do whatever I wanted. So I whipped down my pants, showed them my ass, and said: "See how I've got this double-ass thing going on? This is the part that's going when I win my money!"

The final interview was a panel of fifteen suits in a semi-circle including the head of CBS, Les Moonves, and Mark Burnett, the producer of the show. There was a little seat in the center of the semicircle, so I went inside and said, "Look, you all know you're gonna pick me. What you don't know is that I'm gonna win. And what you need to know for planning purposes is that I'm gonna host next year's show, so can we just move this along?" The room exploded in laughter.

I was in. And I won.

But you know the story about what happened on the island. And you're going to find out my secrets for survival, success, and how to live a happier life. But did being gay help me win *Survivor?*

Absolutely.

Growing up gay, and being openly gay today, has helped me live a much happier life. Not only has it made me more successful, but being part of a minority community, subject to scrutiny by others, has inspired me to be more introspective and forced me to do whatever it takes to understand better who I am. It's also helped me learn what is meaningful about who I am and what matters to me in my life. But being gay has not always been easy.

Some people think that by being gay you get to opt out of some of the traditional roles that heterosexuals face. Nothing could be further from the truth. Not only are gay men generally mistaken for heterosexual men because they feel forced to fit into heterosexual roles in certain environments, but they are often coerced to fit into homosexual roles in other settings. This can be confusing and certainly isn't healthy. My advice: Try to avoid fitting into the boxes that society builds for you.

My earliest sexual experiences had more to do with power than with pleasure. When I was eight years old, I was taken into a little shed behind a house and three older kids stuffed chestnuts up my butt. Two of them held me down while the other stuck them inside me. I remember feeling very helpless and very scared, but I can't recall how I got them out (whether I pulled them out, or pooped them out).

Then, when I was ten, I was molested at the beach by a family friend. We came out of the water after a swim, and he took me into a lifeguard's locker room. He had me stand next to him while he sat naked on the toilet. He was masturbating (I didn't know what he was doing at the time) with my penis in his mouth.

I kept asking him what he was doing, and he kept saying, "Just wait, just wait, you'll see." When he ejaculated I was awestruck. I said, "Oh my God! What is that? Am I going to be able to do that?" Then he asked me if I wanted to put his penis in my mouth, and I said, "No, it would be all salty because we've just been swimming!" It looked like he enjoyed it and nobody found out about it.

I don't recall what happened as a traumatic, life-damaging experience. It was fun and exciting, though strange and a bit shocking. I suppose I could have been bitter or angry about it, but that would have been pointless. It would have hurt and victimized me more than him.

Growing up gay, for me, was a positive experience because it helped me develop certain strengths in the face of adversity. I learned to understand my world in response to being challenged by others—family, classmates, coworkers, and others. What I'm saying, once again, is this: Screw the roles that people have prescribed for you. You don't have to be a victim unless you want to be one. You don't have to carry a chip on your shoulder (another of my survival tips, on page 40) unless that makes you happy, and I don't see how it could.

I don't let roles define me as a person. When I decided to adopt my son Chris, I didn't see myself as a queer man who wanted a kid. I was simply a man who wanted to be a father, just like every other potential father; I just happened to be gay. Before people even know I'm gay, they get to know a little bit about me as a person. That way, we both get to decide, as we're interacting with each other, how that makes each of us feel as individuals.

I think there are far more people who aren't living openly gay lives than there are those who are openly gay. I know there's no way I can quantify that, but I do know that some of these people aren't as happy as they could be. And that's the bottom line. Do what works best for you to make YOU happy.

Yes, I am gay, queer—whatever term you prefer. So what? I gave up caring what other people think about my gayness a long time ago.

I'd prefer you just call me Rich.

CHAPTER THREE

RICH HATCH'S

101 RULES

TO LIVE BY

A h, the moment you've been waiting for. My one hundred and one tips, techniques, and secrets for making a million dollars, losing one hundred pounds, and living a happier life. Now I don't pretend for a moment to have all the answers. But I have had an interesting journey through life so far—but my journey will never really end as long as I continue to learn and grow.

I've overcome a number of issues that many of you might still be dealing with—being broke, being fat, being down on myself. And I have a lot to say about that—I'm a very opinionated person. But much of what you will be able to get from my tips depends on YOUR ability to grow, to learn, and, most importantly, to listen. I've made it my mission to just *listen to people*. And the fact that you've bought this book tells me that you're anxious to hear the secrets of my success. Of course, if you ever want to be able to buy an island or survive on one for thirty-nine days or more, you'll need to understand each and every one of them and be able to apply them in your everyday lives.

HAPPINESS

1

MAKE YOUR OWN HAPPINESS
YOUR TOP PRIORITY.

If you don't, nobody else will.

2

QUIT YOUR PATHETIC JOB.

Jobs and I don't get along. Too many people focus their efforts on getting the kind of job they are supposed to want (doctor, lawyer, stockbroker, internet programmer, etc.) instead of pursuing their passions. Your happiness should be what you're constantly striving for as an individual, not eighty-hour work weeks in a cubicle and a small paycheck. Maybe you're saying you have kids or a mortgage so you can't afford to think only about yourself. Then don't quit your job this second, but make it a point to find time to do something that makes you happy and could lead to a new career or a new source of income.

3

IF AN AREA OF YOUR LIFE REQUIRES CHANGE, DON'T WAIT FOR AN EXCUSE TO TAKE DECISIVE ACTION.

If there's something in your life that you're not happy with, whether you're overweight or you're stuck in a dead-end job, don't wait to be rescued by any power outside of yourself. If you're not happy, do something about it.

4

GET RID OF THAT CHIP ON YOUR SHOULDER.

If you have been victimized, don't victimize yourself a second time by wasting your time and energy fighting stupid fights. That will only empower the person you're angry with and prevent you from living a happy life.

5

THE SKILLS FOR BEING SUCCESSFUL IN BUSINESS ARE THE SAME AS THE SKILLS FOR BEING A SUCCESSFUL PERSON.

Happiness in your life will bring business success.

6

LEARN AS MUCH AS POSSIBLE ABOUT WHATEVER IT IS THAT MAKES YOU HAPPY.

And please don't limit yourself to "the one thing" that makes you happy. Diversify. Find out the reasons behind why something makes you happy and then see if you can find those same elements in other kinds of situations, pursuits, or pastimes. You should have no shortage of things in your life that make you happy. Often they'll be entirely different activities.

7

NEVER LOOK BACK, AT LEAST NOT BEGRUDGINGLY.

Once you learn something that is true, it is impossible to unlearn it. Build upon what you know to be true and don't waste time lamenting over things that might have been.

8

NO ONE EVER GOT RICH (OR HAPPY) BY WORKING NINE-TO-FIVE.

I didn't, which is why I don't. Neither should you, unless you can honestly say that doing so brings you joy.

9

HAPPINESS IS SUCCESS. SUCCESS IS HAPPINESS.

If you're happy, then by definition you're successful. In my mind these words are synonymous with each other.

GETTING TO KNOW YOURSELF

10

IDENTIFY WHAT YOU WANT.

Stop being trapped by living the life that you've ended up in. If you're fed up with how much time you're spending at work, the only person who's going to help you prioritize your time is you.

11

WHATEVER PLANS YOU MAKE, BE FLEXIBLE WITH THEM.

Challenge and change can come from embracing the unexpected. It's often better to change direction when you realize it won't take you where you want to go than to continue along a bad route.

12

WORRY IS A WASTED EMOTION.

Sometimes you don't have control over how you're feeling, but worrying about a situation accomplishes and changes nothing, and it also doesn't enable you to change your circumstances. It makes the bad thing that you're worried about more likely to happen and to continue happening.

13

FOLLOW YOUR PASSIONS.

And make sure that your passions constantly evolve as you grow and evolve.

14

YOU AREN'T DOING ANYTHING IN YOUR LIFE RIGHT NOW THAT YOU DON'T WANT TO BE DOING.

Each of us has the potential inside, right now, to change any-thing about our lives that we don't like. If you don't have a partner and want one, only you have the power to tell yourself: "I'm tired of being single, and I'm going to make a change." If you're lonely, only you can get out there and search for chal-lenging friends. If you're poor, only you can take the initiative to figure out a way to change your situation.

15

IF YOU HAVE A PROBLEM, OR IF THERE'S SOMETHING ABOUT YOURSELF YOU DON'T LIKE, FIRST ACKNOWLEDGE THAT YOU WANT TO BE THAT WAY. THEN ASK YOURSELF, WHY?

When I was three hundred and sixty pounds, I first had to recognize that I wanted to be fat. Then I had to ask myself, why do I want to be fat? What was it about myself that I didn't like that I had to abuse my body in that way? Asking yourself these types of questions will help you understand the real issues behind your problems and lead toward positive change.

16

QUESTION YOURSELF, AND ENJOY QUESTIONING YOURSELF.

And be open to new and surprising answers that will come from listening to and continuing to develop your own unique ideas.

17

AS LONG AS YOU KNOW WHO YOU ARE, IT DOESN'T MATTER WHAT OTHER PEOPLE THINK.

If you're down to earth, well grounded, and know realistically who you are, other people's perceptions of you will never interfere with how you want to live your life.

18

IF YOU DON'T LOVE YOURSELF, CHANGE UNTIL YOU DO.

Pursue an understanding of how others perceive you. Seek out your character flaws and find ways to remedy them. The result of learning to love yourself is that you're much more likely, and much more able, to change what you don't like about yourself.

19

BALANCE ALL OF YOUR NEEDS.

Prioritize the things that you want from your life and the things that are filling up your days and bring balance to your life. To organize your life in a way that maximizes the level of happiness that you can experience, you need to understand where you are, what's going on in your life right now, and what level of effort you are assigning to each aspect of your existence.

20

SELF-AWARENESS IS THE MOST IMPORTANT CATALYST FOR CHANGE.

If you're not aware of who you are or what your potential is, including how you're perceived and how you impact others, then you don't have the tools to recognize how to change.

HEALTH AND FITNESS

21

DIETS DON'T WORK. THEY'RE STUPID.

A diet is only as good as the person who is on it. Forget Jenny Craig, Nutri-System, Weight Watchers. Forget low-fat, high-carb milkshakes. Starving yourself won't make you happy or wealthy or fit. Only when you have a positive mindset, when you have decided you are READY to lose weight and become more physically fit, will you be able to shed those excess pounds and then learn to maintain your fitness and health.

22

BEING FIT AND LOSING EXCESS WEIGHT IS A PRODUCT OF BEING HAPPY AND NOT THE SOURCE OF YOUR HAPPINESS.

I'm not talking about a façade of fitness that's really just skinny-ness, or high school girls looking like Miss Twiggy. Some of the least healthy people I've known are thin. If you can figure out the things that give you joy in life and seek them wholeheartedly, you will do what's needed to prevent your body from being slowed or clogged (both mentally and physically) with excess weight.

23

REDUCE THE AMOUNT OF BREADS, POTATOES, PASTAS, AND SUGAR IN YOUR DAILY DIET.

Since limiting these foods, I've gained energy and feel more alive and aware than ever before in my life. I get most of my carbohydrates from salads, fruits, and vegetables, which I consume in large quantities.

24

DON'T DRINK ALCOHOL, SMOKE CIGARETTES, OR TAKE DRUGS.

These substances are dulling your senses and contribute to a delusional way of looking at life. We've been indoctrinated, in this society, to believe that having a beer or smoking a joint is a good way to relax, that having some wine with dinner or a cigarette at a party is sophisticated and appropriate. I don't know what the long-term effects are, or what else these substances are doing to your body. But why not become, and remain, as aware as you can possibly be? Alcohol, cigarettes, and drugs numb us to challenge and change. You can become more involved with everything around you, and have deeper, more satisfying sensations and experiences without those substances.

25

FOR ME, BEING FAT SUCKED.

Just look at the photos of me in this book. I was almost four hundred pounds at my heaviest. Do I look healthy and happy to you? If you compare the pictures of how I used to look with the cover photo and you're not convinced, then you should look again. Being overweight creates unhappiness, and it is a question of choice. Most overweight people aren't happy and they have made a decision—consciously or unconsciously—to be fat. But just like being overweight is a choice, you can also choose to examine what's going on in your head that's causing you to eat the way you eat, or to live a sedentary lifestyle.

RISK TAKING
AND CHALLENGES

26

ASSESS THE APPROPRIATE LEVEL
OF RISK FOR YOU IN ANY SITUATION.

An action that's risky for one person may not be for another. Asking you to drive one hundred and twenty miles an hour in your car is very different from asking a race car driver to do the same thing. Find a risk that's challenging enough, while offering a reasonable likelihood of success, given your level of expertise.

27

ACCEPT RISK.

In order to change your life, you have to be able to accept a certain element of risk. You have to go from a zone of certainty to one of uncertainty. Between these zones is an area called risk. By accepting risk, you'll either get penalized or rewarded. But if you don't go through that risk, you'll never know if you're able to achieve the ultimate reward. And even if you are penalized, you can always go back and regroup before trying again. Realize that time goes by quickly. Use that to motivate yourself to take a risk. How much time do you want to go by until you try to make a change in your life that could make you happier? Any risk—even if it fails to yield exactly the reward that you hoped it would—is valuable for what you can learn by taking it.

28

EVALUATE THE LIKELIHOOD OF FAILURE BEFORE YOU LET FEAR OF IT GET IN YOUR WAY.

Look at a situation realistically. Weigh the cost of the worst thing that could happen against the benefits of the best thing that could happen. Choose the risks where the value of the positive outcome outweighs what you might lose.

29

ACKNOWLEDGE THAT NOT DOING ANYTHING ALSO HAS A COST.

When you're evaluating possible outcomes, don't forget that not doing anything also carries risk. Weigh the risks involved in waiting versus those associated with moving ahead. Decide whether you really need to make a choice between action and inaction quickly or if you can afford to spend the time to gather more information.

30

ASSESS WHAT IS THE WORST THAT COULD HAPPEN IN A SITUATION YOU'RE AFRAID OF ENTERING.

If you can live with the worst possible result, go forward with all your energy and don't waste time on unproductive worrying.

31

TAKE A CHANCE FOR THE HELL OF IT.

Then take another. When you look back, years and years from now, you'll understand that the biggest risk anyone ever took was to live less than a full life.

32

MAKE AS MANY MISTAKES AS YOU CAN AND MAKE THEM FAST.

Gather as much information as you can through actually doing something, instead of reading or thinking about it. Jump into a situation. Learn from those mistakes and discover what it is that you like and what makes you happy—sometimes by experiencing what you don't like. Don't waste time. When you think about risk, consider that very little that you're ever likely to encounter is life-threatening. When you've learned from these mistakes, move on.

33

SET YOUR LIMITS.

If you're dissatisfied with long hours at work and you still haven't quit your pathetic job, then at least set your limits on how much you're willing to do. Do something courageous the next time you're expected to stay after five. Do as much as you can with your eight-hour day, and then leave right at five o'clock. You'll be amazed at how other people respond to you once you've clearly defined what you ARE and AREN'T willing to do.

34

CONFRONTATION IS A GOOD THING.

It is at the core of honesty and can help you ascertain the truth in a given situation.

CHALLENGING YOURSELF

35

CHANGE YOUR ROUTINE.

Throughout this book I've stressed the importance of challenging yourself. How do you do that? You start by changing your routine. This isn't easy. There's a good reason why people fall into a rut: Ruts are easy. That's why doing something different will seem difficult, strenuous, or not worth the effort. But if you're in a rut, you owe it to yourself to get out of it by taking a risk. And, once again, ask yourself: What's the worst thing that could happen?

36

IN ORDER TO ACHIEVE ANY GOAL, YOU MUST HAVE CLARITY AND DESIRE.

The first step toward achieving a goal is being clear-sighted enough to realize that there IS something bigger and better out there for you. If you look around, you can see such awareness in successful and happy people. Instead of being envious, realize that you too can have that success and happiness. Ask yourself: How am I going to get there? Once you've defined what it is that you want, enact the desire that you already have. That desire in fact helped you realize you could have this success that's been eluding you. Then carry out the steps necessary to transform your vision into reality.

37

QUESTION THE DIRECTION YOUR LIFE IS GOING AND PUT YOURSELF IN THE MOST CHALLENGING SITUATIONS YOU CAN.

When you identify people you can learn from, and they point to things about you that are problematic, thank them for having done so. Then, figure out whether you agree with their assessment. Do something about it if you do, and then move on and look for other things you could improve about yourself.

38

CHALLENGE YOURSELF DIFFERENTLY.

I'm not talking about becoming a workaholic. I'm talking about challenging yourself differently, because by doing so, you can't help but learn. If you're used to challenging yourself in a particular way, and maybe to you that means working ten hours a day, well, you're not challenging yourself at all. You're doing the same thing over and over, and you're probably learning very little. To challenge yourself would be to go to work for an hour, and take the rest of the day off when you know you have work to do.

39

SEEING THE BIG FISH DOES NOT NECESSARILY MEAN CATCHING THE BIG FISH.

I'm not talking sting rays here. I'm talking about goals, whether in business or in your personal life, and how you go about achieving them. It's useless to set goals and then NOT challenge yourself to achieve them. Challenging yourself to reach the goals that you set is the best way to make sure your risk will pay off in reward.

40

OVERCOME FUNCTIONAL FIXEDNESS.

Have you ever used a screwdriver to open a can of paint? Well, why did you do that? A screwdriver is made to turn screws, not to open cans of paint. Oh, but it was available, and it worked! Good for you! You've just overcome your functional fixedness by picking up a screwdriver as opposed to driving to a hardware store and picking up a paint can opener. Most people are functionally fixed about things and people in their lives every single day. If I'm walking down the hall toward you at work and I think to myself, "Oh, here comes that jerk I don't like," and avoid you at all costs, I believe our next interaction is going to repeat prior negative interactions. How responsible am I for the way you interact with me? Well, what if I challenged you differently and you interact with me positively? So make an effort to challenge yourself. You never know what you may discover about yourself and the people around you.

41

YOU'RE NOT A MENIAL PERSON EVEN IF YOU'RE DOING A MENIAL JOB.

If you truly believe you're not meant for something better, you'll never achieve something better. And if you're happy doing what you are doing, then there is nothing better.

42

ASK QUESTIONS AND LISTEN TO THE ANSWERS.

The most challenging thing you can do is to listen to another human being. Just listen. You will be amazed by what you can learn.

43

IF IT REALLY IS YOUR "ONLY" VICE, GET RID OF IT.

I hear this one a lot. Yeah, smoking's my only vice, drinking's my only vice, eating's my only vice. And don't we deserve at least one thing in our lives that makes us "happy"? Well that's the problem. Vices, by their definition, cannot make you happy. Vices make it easier for you to be less successful. It's that ONE vice that's holding you back, weighing you down, and keeping you from what you really want in life. So challenge yourself. Drop that vice. Help yourself get happy.

44

PUT YOUR FAITH IN YOURSELF TO CHANGE YOUR LIFE, AND STOP WAITING FOR CHANGE TO COME FROM SOMEWHERE ELSE.

People are often looking for the quick fix to change their lives—the winning lottery ticket, the big inheritance. The truth is that there is no quick fix. You CAN change your life and make it better. You can become happier. But it won't happen unless you are willing to take the first step toward success yourself.

45

POTENTIAL IS
UNEXPLORED POSSIBILITY.

It's what people could be capable of if they were challenged to meet a goal.

46

NOBODY CAN DRAG YOU DOWN
EXCEPT YOURSELF.

Carefully consider your thoughts and work tirelessly to eradicate negative thought patterns. These harmful patterns, which often linger from childhood stresses or trauma, can prevent you from growing and changing. Work through these problems in any way you can, talk about them, think through each detail, each feeling, each event. Doing so can change your life.

47

TREAT EACH NEW PERSON WHOM YOU MEET EQUALLY.

You can't form an opinion about a person without any information. But once you meet someone, you should be able to determine fairly quickly where that person will start to fit into your personal hierarchy. Along with this hierarchy should be a differentiation as to how you will plan to invest your time with new people whom you meet.

48

EFFORT INVESTED IN THINKING BEFORE TAKING ACTION IS WORTH IT.

But don't let thinking something through prevent you from acting.

49

CONQUER IT BY DOING IT.

This seems like an easy one, but it's important. Learn something by actually doing it. Get off your ass and take a chance. Stop making excuses and stop listening to the excuses other people are making for you. You're not going to learn about your limits unless you test them. In the grand scheme of things, whether you're sixteen years old or sixty, you'll be tree food soon enough. So put down this book and go challenge yourself differently. Learn something. Happy trails. Read the rest later.

50

EYE CONTACT IS IMPORTANT.

Most of what people perceive as honest or real in communication is transmitted nonverbally, compared with much smaller percentages through the tone of your voice or the words actually spoken. If you're telling someone, "Yeah, it's really great to meet you," and you're staring at the wall behind them, you're not going to make a lasting impression, and you're not going to be able to engage them on any level that's meaningful. Take more responsibility for what you communicate to others by considering and acknowledging what you're saying nonverbally. And deal more honestly with what others are actually saying to you.

51

LISTENING IS EVERYTHING.

But you must be an active listener. Challenge and engage whomever it is that you're communicating with to ensure that the message intended is the same one you're receiving. This is the basis for effective communication.

FRIENDSHIP

52

AN HONEST FRIENDSHIP IS THE ONLY FRIENDSHIP WORTH HAVING.

It allows both people to trust and be truthful, go through times of disagreement, and offer each other the potential to change and grow.

53

UNDERSTAND WHAT LOYALTY MEANS TO YOU.

Do you want to be on time for a friend who is always late? Do you want to protect a friend who gets drunk and acts in ways that you don't condone? Do you want to listen to someone who knows less about a subject than you do when that person is not willing to listen to you? Challenge yourself on these kinds of issues so that you understand how you're acting with your friends and why.

54

WHEN YOU'RE INTERACTING WITH OTHERS, EVALUATE THE OTHER PERSON'S ABILITY TO UNDERSTAND WHAT YOU'RE DOING AND SAYING.

Don't change what you do to please another person, but make sure that your intended message is being received as clearly as possible so that you can achieve your desired outcome.

55

IT'S MORE IMPORTANT TO SHOW YOUR FEELINGS THROUGH ACTIONS THAN IT IS TO EXPRESS THEM VERBALLY.

Words like "sorry" or "love" have been abused by people for so long that they have lost almost all meaning. Show people you love them through your actions of caring and commitment, and challenge them to do the same. Prove that you're sorry by not repeating past errors or infractions.

56

FIND FRIENDS WHO CHALLENGE YOU; AND WHEN THEY STOP CHALLENGING YOU, FIND NEW FRIENDS.

There's no better way to find out about yourself than by finding a person who knows more than you do. Become valuable to that person in whatever ways you can. Ask that person to challenge you. Think about that person's suggestions. Take advice. Take risks. Take chances. See what you learn. When you stop learning from someone, that person is no longer your friend. Accept that reality and move on.

57

EXAMINE HOW YOU DEFINE THE WORD "FRIEND."

For me, this word defines a person in my life who is very close to me—someone who deals honestly with me and interacts with me in ways that help each of us understand the other. A friend is someone who's loyal, dependable, honest, and—most of all—challenging. True friends tell you what they think and not what they think you want to hear. If you don't have friends, if you've surrounded yourself with acquaintances who only engage you in pleasant cocktail-hour conversations, ask yourself: Am I really ready to grow as a person?

58

WHEN THINKING ABOUT SEVERING A RELATIONSHIP WITH A FRIEND BECAUSE YOU BELIEVE THAT PERSON HAS WRONGED YOU, UNDERSTAND THAT PEOPLE ARE HUMAN, AND INTEGRATE THAT LESSON INTO A MUCH BIGGER PICTURE.

People are flawed (yes, even you); for me, it isn't the end of a relationship when somebody impacts me negatively. I look at who that person is and ask myself what caused the discord, and then I prepare myself for it happening again IF I decide that the value of the friendship outweighs the wrong committed. I also consider whether something in my view of myself needs to be changed, and whether I've contributed in some way to the strain in the relationship.

59

FIND A COMPATIBLE PARTNER (OR A COMPATIBLE FRIEND). BUT **NEVER** SETTLE FOR SOMEONE OUT OF DESPERATION.

When you're looking for a partner or a friend, listen closely and make evaluations. If you decide someone isn't right for you, move on quickly—that way you'll find someone who is right for you that much sooner.

60

CHALLENGE PEOPLE TO TELL YOU WHAT THEY'RE REALLY THINKING ON A REGULAR BASIS.

This is not an easy thing to do, especially if you're not in the habit of challenging people's assertions. But this is the best way I know to start learning how you are perceived by others. And then start questioning their perceptions. This person feels this and that person feels that. Ask yourself: Is that accurate? Do I feel that way about myself? Should I?

61

FIND PEOPLE WHO ARE EXPERTS AT SPECIFIC THINGS AND LEARN TO UTILIZE INFORMATION FROM THEM.

Figure out whom you can trust, and get help from them. You can't do it alone.

ROMANCE

62

DECIDE HOW INTIMACY AND SEXUALITY IMPACT YOU BEFORE YOU ENGAGE IN EITHER.

Different people have different relationships with their body, with their sexuality, even with their ability to be naked in front of other people. Before you get involved physically or emotionally with a person, see if your levels of intimacy and sexuality are in tune with one another.

63

CHALLENGE THOSE YOU LOVE.

Help them understand who THEY are. And love only those who are willing to be challenged. If you are my friend and I challenge you, and if you aren't interested in, or willing to meet, that challenge, then I learn that you aren't somebody who's challenging enough for me. You won't ever be able to tell me truthfully what you're thinking about anything.

HONESTY

64

ACKNOWLEDGE WHEN YOU'VE SCREWED SOMETHING UP.

You're not apologizing for anything here, but you're aware that you did something that, if you had the chance to do again, you might approach differently. By owning up to a mistake instead of trying to get off the hook with a vacant apology, you're acknowledging a process at work. That process tells the person you are committed to not making the same mistake twice.

65

LEARN HOW TO JUDGE
YOUR OWN LIMITATIONS.

Taking calculated chances is a good way to start. Nothing is gained by delusional and inflated ideas about your abilities. Be realistic and strive to lessen what limitations you realistically perceive.

66

DIPLOMAS AND DEGREES
WON'T MAKE YOU A BETTER PERSON.

I could not give a hoot about what college you went to or what degree you have. Our society puts too much emphasis on spending an enormous amount of money on getting a label to stick after your name or an overpriced diploma to hang on your wall. This gives people a false sense of success because degrees have nothing to do with how intelligent you are or how much you can achieve in life. So if you don't have a fancy degree, relax, because it's not going to get in the way of your success. And if you do have one of those fancy diplomas, don't let that false sense of success fool you into thinking you're all set.

67

BEING HONEST IS THE MOST COMPASSIONATE THING ONE CAN DO FOR ANOTHER HUMAN BEING.

Politeness and insincere compliments are not compassionate ways to treat another person. Compassion is about helping people understand what you really think about them even at the cost of what they'll think about you. Honesty helps you learn more about other people, which will help you grow as a person.

68

STOP PRETENDING TO BE SO DAMNED POLITE. IN FACT, JUST STOP PRETENDING.

Being polite is being dishonest. It prevents people from interacting with each other in ways that are real, honest, and meaningful. While you're sitting there at a cocktail party talking about "Isn't Jim's Beemer great?" and "Wasn't that party in the Hamptons the *most* fabulous?" you're taking time away from engaging in meaningful conversation where you might actually learn something, either about the person you're talking to or about yourself. Say something real and see where that takes you.

69

DON'T TRUST NICE PEOPLE.
THEY'RE NOT NICE.

For your own success and happiness, contemplate YOUR feelings about what somebody said or did or how a person is reacting to what you have said or done. Then respond to that feeling honestly.

70

TAKE MORE RESPONSIBILITY
FOR WHAT YOU ARE ACTUALLY
COMMUNICATING TO OTHERS.

If you're not engaging someone, either by avoiding eye contact, or by not listening to the person, be honest by acknowledging that this person is less valuable to you, and recognize that's what you're doing.

71

IF YOU MEET ANOTHER HONEST PERSON THAT YOU'D LIKE TO GET TO KNOW BETTER, SAY SOMETHING HONEST ABOUT THEM.

You'll intrigue them, and you'll encourage that person to be more honest about what he or she wants from you.

72

THE VIRTUE IN YOUR ACTIONS LIES IN HOW HONEST YOU ARE TO OTHERS ABOUT WHO YOU ARE, AND TO YOURSELF ABOUT WHAT YOU WANT.

73

DEAL MORE HONESTLY WITH WHAT PEOPLE ARE ACTUALLY SAYING TO YOU BOTH VERBALLY AND THROUGH BODY LANGUAGE.

When someone isn't engaging you, by not listening to you or by avoiding eye contact, that person is saying that you aren't valued. That should NOT be okay with you.

74

IF YOU CAN'T BE HONEST WITH SOMEBODY, THEN YOU DON'T HAVE A HEALTHY RELATIONSHIP WITH YOURSELF.

You're not aware of who you are and the fact that you're really just one step away from being eaten by trees (i.e., dead). So do yourself a favor and find out why you have a hard time telling the truth to someone you care about.

75

SECRETS ARE IMPRISONING.

Try not to keep them.

76

IF YOU'RE SHY, SNAP OUT OF IT!

Shyness is right up there with politeness on my list of characteristics you should get rid of. Being shy isn't honest, and it isn't even real. If you're not happy with yourself, change right now. But never get embarrassed, never be nervous around anyone. These things just waste time because, like politeness, they inhibit honest and genuine interaction.

77

THINK ABOUT REAL CHANGE BEFORE YOU APOLOGIZE TO ANYONE FOR ANYTHING.

I will not apologize for honesty. You shouldn't either. But when I find that I haven't been honest, I try to figure out why and to make whatever adjustments are necessary within myself in order to have the strength to be honest the next time.

LOOKING OUT FOR NUMERO UNO

78

SELFISHNESS IS A VIRTUE.

Sounds selfish, doesn't it? Well, any time you're looking at what's going to benefit you, and you pursue that honestly, you get closer to being happy and you impact your environment and the people around you in positive ways. For example, if you give somebody a gift, it's because you want that good feeling that comes to you from the act of making someone you care about happy. You may be making somebody happy, but you also want to feel happy yourself. Being selfish can be a way of helping yourself while helping others. You can't help other people or give them what they want until you know who YOU are and what YOU want.

79

START THE PROCESS OF LOVING YOURSELF.

Become more aware of who you are. Don't think that you already know how people really feel about you. You probably don't. If you think you do, if you think you have all the answers, then you're not in a position to grow and develop.

80

LEARN HOW TO GET COMFORTABLE ENOUGH WITH YOURSELF TO REALIZE THAT YOU STILL HAVE A LOT TO LEARN ABOUT YOURSELF AND OTHER PEOPLE.

If you're comfortable in your own skin and willing to be judgmental (i.e., honest), you open yourself up to the possibility of change.

81

UNDERSTAND THE GAME YOU'RE PLAYING, WHATEVER IT IS.

Question your reality, and make sure that you understand how you're impacted by the things you're doing.

82

BE EGOCENTRIC.

You are what you think. If you don't spend enough time thinking about YOU, and understanding you, and understanding your own perspective, you can't know when you're truly happy. For me, being "egocentric" means focusing on myself, which I think is a good thing. Spend an inordinate amount of time on yourself.

SURVIVING IN YOUR OWN (AND OTHERS') ENVIRONMENT

83

LEARN WHAT YOU WANT FROM SOMEBODY ELSE AND NOT WHAT SOMEBODY ELSE WANTS FROM YOU.

If you're in a situation such as a job interview or if you're out on a date, figure out what you want from the other person and not what they want from you. Don't waste your time trying to package yourself as somebody you think other people will like. Know exactly why you are in the situation, what you want to get from it, and be ready to face challenges or questions regarding your identity.

84

IF YOU'RE PART OF A TEAM, FIGURE OUT WHO **YOU** ARE AND WHAT YOU WANT BEFORE EXAMINING THE OTHER MEMBERS.

Teams are a part of everyday life. For a team to be effective, whether it's a company, a family, or a bunch of strangers stranded on a deserted island, all members must know who they are, what they are capable of, and how they are impacting the other people around them. Work on knowing who you are and how you fit in.

85

LEARN HOW TO SET UP YOUR OWN RULES WITHIN THE CONSTRAINTS OF A RIGOROUS ENVIRONMENT.

You don't have to conform. If you keep focused on who you are, you can figure out ways to retain your identity in any environment.

86

LEARN THE RULES OF WHATEVER GAME YOU'RE PLAYING.

Understand the rules and challenge the limits. If you apply the rules from one situation to a situation where a different set of rules are called for, you're going to get left behind by people who ALREADY understand what the new rules are. So instead of getting left behind, get THEM to teach you the rules if you don't already know what they are.

87

BUILD ALLIANCES.

Protect the people with whom you've invested time and energy. They're worth it. Respect them. Be loyal to them. Challenge them and listen to their challenges. Encourage them to be successful, and they will encourage you to be successful.

88

FOR A DECISION TO BE MEANINGFUL, IT HAS TO BE INFORMED.

Whether you're trying to decide who you want to vote in as president of your country, or who you want to vote off your island, or even whether it's okay for your son or daughter to stay out past curfew, you need to gather as much information as is necessary to make an intelligent decision. Protect your interests (including your children) without undermining them.

89

ACTIVE OBSERVATION IS THE KEY TO SUCCESS.

It doesn't matter what the goal is at hand. As long as you're observing—people, places, things—you're growing, and if you're growing, by definition you will be successful.

FINANCIAL FREEDOM

90

FOCUS ON THOUGHTS RATHER THAN THINGS.

For a man who's now a "millionaire" I don't have a lot of wants. I want enough to live comfortably, but I don't want to live excessively. I want a nice house, but I don't need an eighteen-room mansion. Focusing on the material things you acquire BEYOND what you need to live comfortably doesn't allow you to grow as a person because your happiness and therefore your success becomes dependent on things and NOT on YOURSELF.

91

IF YOU'RE A HOMEOWNER, EXAMINE THE PROPERTY YOU OWN TO FIND UNTAPPED POTENTIAL.

Are you living on your property, given your current circumstances, in as intelligent a way as possible? Do you have a second floor where you could house a college student and earn an extra five hundred dollars a month? Do you have an empty space in a three-car garage that you could rent to someone who wants to store a car there? Again, the key is being flexible.

92

GIVE YOURSELF A RAISE. BUY A HOUSE.

The first house I ever purchased was a four-bedroom, two-bath house outside of Washington, D.C., for $128,000. I lived in one bedroom and rented out the other three. So I had enough to cover my mortgage, paid no rent, and was building equity in the house. You can earn money from buying a house by being open-minded, flexible, and NOT functionally fixed (see that secret on page 62).

93

THINK YOUR WAY OUT OF POVERTY INSTEAD OF TRYING TO WORK YOUR WAY OUT OF IT.

Should you be focusing on just making money? When you have enough money to support yourself and your family, how do you go beyond that? Once you've conquered subsistence, use any extra time to decide what makes you happy and pursue that on a regular basis.

94

HIRE A BRILLIANT ACCOUNTANT SO YOU DON'T LOSE EVERY PENNY YOU HAVE TO UNCLE SAM.

You've earned it and you want to protect it. Nothing wrong with that. Always get the best professional help you can, whether it's an accountant, a lawyer, a financial planner, or an insurance broker. Know what you need from them before asking for advice and check references carefully.

REINVENTING THE RULES

95

BE DIFFERENT.

By being different, by finding your own voice, developing your own ideas, you can begin to visualize solutions that other people won't be able to see. I find that people who are different are more interested in improving or changing the way things are done. This is often exactly the attitude that's needed to solve a difficult problem.

96

CRAWL OUT OF THE BOXES THAT PEOPLE TRY TO SQUEEZE YOU INTO.

Such boxes are dead ends. To develop your own talents, find your own passions, and build your own identity, you have to move beyond the expectations of others.

97

EXPLORE YOUR SEXUAL IDENTITY. DON'T LET OTHER PEOPLE DEFINE IT FOR YOU.

You are uniquely you. Be proud of it. Don't apologize for who you are. Just love and express your sexual self with happiness and intensity.

98

BREAK SOME RULES.

One of the most important rules in life is knowing when to break them. This is what challenge is all about.

99

EMBRACE YOUR IMAGINATION.

Take the time to explore the ways you think differently as opposed to the ways you've been told you're SUPPOSED to think by whomever—people at work, your parents, society in general—in short, the constraints of being subject to a particular paradigm. If you embrace your imagination, and if you allow yourself to consider ideas outside the scope of societal constraints, you're likely to come up with ways in which you could become happier.

100

YOU'LL NEVER KNOW YOUR LIMITS UNTIL YOU FAIL.

So fail, learn from failing, and try again and again until you learn what you have to do in order to succeed at whatever it is that you decide YOU want to do.

101

YOU'VE GOT A LOT TO LEARN, JUST LIKE ME.

But let's work together, let's think more, question more, listen better, watch more closely. Only then can we all improve ourselves, challenge and be challenged by our friends, and live a happier, more fulfilled, life.

CHAPTER FOUR

RICH'S PHOTO LOG

Me in 2nd grade, 1968.
I'm seven years old.

Yearbook photo, 1979.

Me and Maureen, my prom date. We got engaged a year later.
Needless to say, it fell through.

West Point Preparatory, 1982.

Graduation Day, West Point Prep, 1982.
Me and my grandma, grandpa, and my two sisters.

Me and my mom.

My father, at graduation day, found a raccoon foraging in a garbage can. So he pulled him right out!

West Point, 1983.

A fresh young plebe at West Point.

Me in my fatigues, West Point, 1982. I'm in great shape here.

Dating at West Point.

Me and my grandma.

Bartending in Virginia, March 1987.

Me and my partner, Ralph.

Here I am, at
almost 250 pounds,
in Lake Tahoe. It's
no accident I'm
posed next to the
"Tahoe Queen"!

My friends, Warren, Andy, Patrick, and Dan, 1996.

My great friend Tom, and my son Chris.

Chris, the summer I adopted him, 1997.

Taking some sun with my friend Kathleen.

That's ME? Almost 360 pounds in 1997, with my son Chris.

Fishing for halibut in Alaska.

Starting out with a group of new friends on a camping trip
in Alaska. I've always enjoyed these types of trips.

Enjoying the brisk outdoors in Alaska.

Me and some friends on my camping trip to Alaska.

Alaska, with my shirt off. I don't feel cold at all!

CHAPTER FIVE

DAMN RIGHT

I WON!

(And What You Can Do
After Achieving Your Goals)

Sure I won. I survived a thirty-nine-day camping trip that fifty million people watched on television and I won a million dollars. No more, no less. So what happens after an experience like *Survivor*? Or more importantly, how do you deal with achieving a goal that you've worked hard to attain? A lot of what this book has dealt with is how to challenge yourself to achieve the goals that work best for you. But I haven't spent a lot of time talking about how to deal with what to do after you have reached that goal.

This is important to me, because achieving your goals will bring up a new set of conditions, a host of new challenges. Now that I've quit smoking, how do I challenge myself to fill that time with something that isn't a vice? Now that I've lost the weight that I want to lose, how do I challenge myself to keep that weight from coming back?

I hope that by sharing how I dealt with what happened to me after *Survivor*, how I handled the aftermath of achieving a personal goal, you'll be able to learn not only how to deal with achieving your own personal goals but also what to do once you've attained them.

The show's wrap party was held in the camp built to house the crew, behind the tribal counsel set. All I ate was a couple of strange-looking white burgers, even though I was absolutely starving. I was so mentally exhausted that I didn't have the energy to dive into the skewered pork, fish heads, and piles of unrecognizable Malaysian food. Screw the food. Screw partying late into the night. I took a shower, and went to bed.

At about six the next morning, I hopped up on a boat leaving the island. On the way back to Borneo, I had some time to myself just to think. I was in an evaluative state, because I had just gotten the best rest I had had in a long while. I was exhausted in every possible way from the past thirty-nine days, but I was happy to be relieved of a lot of that stress, that mental anxiety. I was sitting on the boat and asking myself: How do I feel? What did I feel the night before, in the midst of achieving my goal, and how did I feel after having achieved it? And most importantly, I was asking myself: What did I learn? The answer: Nothing earth-shattering! Thinking back on it, I believe the experience gave me an increased confidence in my ability to observe human behavior and a realistic perspective on those observations. I began to anticipate the future—seeing my son again, talking to friends about things other than the show. . . . But first I had to rest more and eat.

At the resort in mainland Borneo, I still didn't eat like a maniac. But I felt an incredible craving—not for meat or bread—simply for fruit. And the fruit was beautiful. I ate mangos and papayas, pineapples and lychee nuts (they look like eyeballs, but they're delicious!). It was pure pleasure.

Asking myself what I've learned, and what I feel after I achieve a goal is something I'm constantly doing. Only by analyzing the answers you give yourself to these questions can you grow as an individual and get yourself ready to move on to the next challenge. I thought about what was on the minds of the other contestants. I thought about what it would take for me to remain the same person after my victory in front of fifty-two million viewers, recognizing that though it would increase opportunities it wouldn't change who I am. The one thing that had changed dramatically was my weight and I wanted to find concrete ways to keep it off. Since leaving the island, I've gone running, sometimes VERY slowly, almost every day. And I AM keeping the weight off. It's a priority.

I didn't spend as much time as I would have liked, right after leaving the island, trying to figure out answers to the many complex questions I had, because I was focusing on the secret I'd have to keep for the next four months. Since it was a closed set on the final day of shooting, few people knew the outcome of the game. I couldn't talk with ANYONE about what had happened.

So I started to ask myself how I was going to interact with other people knowing what I knew, and I began to prepare myself to remain aware that I wasn't going to share what had happened with anyone. I asked myself: How am I going to do that? I was evaluating why it was important to me to interact with people the way I was planning to interact with them and what would make me happy about that. I realized that everyone whom I cared about would be that much more excited when they found out I DID win, along with everybody else who faithfully watched the show.

I was planning the next phase of my life. And I recommend this to everybody. As long as evaluating your choices doesn't prevent you from actually making a choice, evaluate what choices you have so you can make the best decisions possible given the available information.

Back home, I was surprised at how easy it was not to tell anyone the secret. I don't think it crossed my mind even once. The premise of the show only worked IF you didn't know who was going to take home the prize. And the premise, when it was first described to me, seemed designed to challenge television viewers, and I believe that most people like to be challenged. When I went in for my interview at CBS, I told them this show was going to be the biggest hit they ever had. People would be able to watch other people interact in a real and challenging way, project onto these people what they wanted, guess at the outcome, try to figure things out ahead of time, and manage the unpredictability of it all.

But most importantly, the show was real. You could watch how people handled situations and relationships that weren't con-cocted. This show wasn't scripted and there was a lot at stake. People's real selves, both on the island, and watching at home on TV, got pushed, got challenged. This was a mentally demanding social experiment. The skills I've shared with you were the tools I used to achieve my goal—being observant, being aware, being interested in people's perceptions about who they are, and cultivating a natural curiosity for trying to discover more about people.

And it is important to love yourself—to build the confidence NOT to believe the voices in society that tell you: You're not a good person unless you have the perfect body. You're not a good person unless you have the right clothes. You're not a good person unless you have the perfect job. These kinds of attitudes are damaging, destructive, and have absolutely nothing to do with either happiness or success.

One of the most fascinating things I've learned in all of this is that people love a winner even more than they love an underdog. When people saw that I had certain advantages over other players on the island (just as they had other advantages over me, whether it was their strength or their youth), people reacted to me very negatively. Many people hated me before I won, because they didn't fully understand that they were watching a game. After discovering that I had won, and scrutinizing how and why that happened, people have been overwhelmingly supportive.

Personally, I'm not affected by either swing of the pendulum. I love me. Going from someone whom nobody knew to someone that everybody knows has had almost no impact on me. The thing that HAS changed, in addition to my weight, is the way other people act toward me.

Peoples' perceptions of me are always going to be somewhat different from who I actually am. And if I live my life, or am impacted by peoples' perceptions of me in such a strong way as to change the way I live my life, then I have a problem. I've learned that it just doesn't matter what other people say or think about you as long as YOU know who you are.

And I know who I am. Going on *Survivor* wasn't about proving anything to anyone. And utilizing my survival secrets should not be about proving anything to anyone except yourself. Set a goal to live a happier life, pure and simple. Then challenge yourself to achieve it.

CHAPTER SIX

WHAT I'M GOING TO DO WITH MY LIFE AND WHAT YOU CAN DO WITH YOURS

"**S**o what the hell are you going to do now, Rich?" You know, a lot of people have been asking me what's the next challenge for Rich Hatch. I have a lot of people to help me manage what my next moves will be—a literary agent, a lecture agent, a manager, a general agency, a publicist, and so on. Why so many people? Well, my publicist deals with all of my press. If a television show wants to have me on to discuss my book, or if somebody wants to interview me for a newspaper or a magazine, the publicist keeps track of the types of things that will keep me visible. My agent handles requests for commercials, movies, and television programs. And in the midst of all of this, my manager decides what moves are most appropriate for me and makes sure that I don't make bad choices.

Having all of these people working for me could be overwhelming, but I look at it a little differently. These people are skilled professionals and they provide me with information that helps me make decisions. It's a hectic world for me right now—Annie Leibowitz just did a photo shoot of me for *Vanity Fair*, interviewers ask me questions while I'm in a limousine on my way from one TV show guest appearance to the next. Being famous is a fascinating and illuminating experience. It would be very easy to get swallowed up by it if I started to believe the hype about myself.

I'm not interested in that. What I'm interested in is happiness. And taking risks. My life is, and will continue to be, a series of risks. And I'd like to make other people happy. So when people ask me what am I going to do now that I'm a millionaire . . . well, pretty much the same things I was doing before I won the money, or before a single episode of *Survivor* aired.

I will use the money for pretty much the same kinds of things that you would have used it for if you had won a million dollars. I'm going to pay off some bills. I'm going to fix up my house, which is what I was doing before I left for the island (although now I can fix it up a little faster than I could before). I'm going to pay off some of my mortgage. Some of the money will go to Uncle Sam. I plan to use some of my new-found celebrity and resources to restart the

Horizon Bound program or something similar to it, and with Reebok's help (plug, plug) I think this may be a little closer to reality. Finally, I'm going to provide a better life for my son. Although I'm sure many of you would like further details about how Chris and I are doing, I've decided not to involve him in my public life any further. I'll say simply again that I'm a loving father and that Chris is doing very well.

There is a selfish goal that I'd like to pursue. I've been tossing it around in my head since long before I went on the show. There's a small island in Narragansett Bay I'd like to buy. Its proximity is appealing, and its size (sixteen acres) would make it ideal for me. I would love my own island. I'd landscape it with beautiful paths, private gardens, patios, beaches . . . the island would become my personal paradise.

Would there be any games on my island? You bet. We'd play Balderdash. Are you familiar with it? You start out with words, and people give definitions to these words and you try to make the other people believe that your definition is more accurate. You'd like it. It's a game where you bluff people in order to win.

I don't know how long all of this is going to last. So for now I'm just going to continue to live a life where my one goal is to challenge myself to grow and evolve. And I know I'm going to get there. Knowing that there's so much more out there for me, and also for you with these survival secrets in hand, makes me excited, for all of our futures.

That knowledge and the journey ahead make me happy. How about you?